Frankl's "Thorn Patch" Fieldbook

as told to Philip Ramsey

Pegasus Communications, Inc.
Waltham

Acquiring editor: Kellie Wardman O'Reilly
Project editor: Lauren Johnson
Interior design: Robert Lowe and Lainie Rutkow
Production: Lainie Rutkow
Cover illustration and figures on pp. 11 and 13: Robin Runci Mazo

♻ Printed on recycled paper.
Printed in the United States of America.
First printing August 1997

ISBN 1-883823-21-8

Pegasus Communications, Inc.
One Moody Street
Waltham, MA 02453-5339
Phone: 781-398-9700
Fax: 781-894-7175
www.pegasuscom.com

5168

04 03 02 01 00 99   10 9 8 7 6 5 4

Contents

Publications by Pegasus Communications, Inc.

Anthologies
Managing the Rapids: Stories from the Forefront of the Learning Organization
Reflections on Creating Learning Organizations
The New Workplace: Transforming the Character and Culture of Our Organizations
Organizational Learning at Work: Embracing the Challenges of the New Workplace
Making It Happen: Stories from Inside the New Workplace

The Pegasus Workbook Series
Systems Archetype Basics: From Story to Structure
Systems Thinking Basics: From Concepts to Causal Loops

The "Billibonk" Series
Billibonk & the Thorn Patch
Frankl's "Thorn Patch" Fieldbook
Billibonk & the Big Itch
Frankl's "Big Itch" Fieldbook

Learning Fables
Outlearning the Wolves: Surviving and Thriving in a Learning Organization
Shadows of the Neanderthal: Illuminating the Beliefs That Limit Our Organizations

Human Dynamics
Human Dynamics: A New Framework for Understanding People and Realizing the Potential in Our Organizations

The Innovations in Management Series
From Mechanistic to Social Systemic Thinking: A Digest of a Talk by Russell L. Ackoff
Applying Systems Archetypes
Toward Learning Organizations: Integrating Total Quality Control and Systems Thinking
Designing a Systems Thinking Intervention: A Strategy for Leveraging Change
The Natural Step: A Framework for Achieving Sustainability in Our Organizations
Anxiety in the Workplace: Using Systems Thinking to Deepen Understanding
The Soul of Corporate Leadership: Guidelines for Values-Centered Governance
Creating Sustainable Organizations: Meeting the Economic, Ecological, and Social Challenges of the 21st Century
Creating Value: Linking the Interests of Customers, Employees, and Investors
Relinking Life and Work: Toward a Better Future
Facing the Competition: An Organization Mobilizes for Large-Scale Change
Organizational Change at Philips Display Components: Reflections on a Learning Journey
Introduction to Systems Thinking
Rebounding, Rebuilding, Renewing at Shell Oil: A Former CEO Reflects on Large-Scale Change

The Toolbox Reprint Series
Systems Archetypes I: Diagnosing Systemic Issues and Designing High-Leverage Interventions
Systems Archetypes II: Using Systems Archetypes to Take Effective Action
Systems Thinking Tools: A User's Reference Guide

Newsletters
THE SYSTEMS THINKER™
LEVERAGE:® *News and Ideas for the Organizational Learner*

Welcome to My Fieldbook!

Hey! Welcome to my Fieldbook. I'm glad you've read the story of *Billibonk & the Thorn Patch*. It was fun for me to help Billibonk while he was learning about life in the jungle—I got to learn plenty, too. In this Fieldbook, I get to do the same thing with you: help you find out how some of the lessons Billibonk and I learned can be useful to what you do. So, if Billibonk can get out of a thorn patch, you should be able to work out why some of your organization's problems seem especially thorny, and decide how to get out of them and *stay* out.

As you work through the Fieldbook, keep in mind that during my adventures with Billibonk—especially at the beginning, when he wasn't used to listening to small animals—I had to yell at him to get him to pay attention. Sometimes the lessons we were learning were a bit painful for him—or he didn't *want* to learn them! Likewise, at times some of the questions in this Fieldbook might be a bit difficult for you to think about. Good! The more painful they are, the more important they must be.

The Fieldbook is organized so that you can do several things:
- Understand what organizational learning is, and decide whether it is important for you and your organization.
- Think about how the lessons Billibonk learned might apply to you.
- Find out how to use these lessons to plan actions that will make a difference for your organization or team.

Happy learning!

—Frankl 🐾

What Is Organizational Learning?

Organizational learning is about people wanting to achieve certain results, and depending on each other for this to happen. Learning is a wonderful thing, and it seems to be a normal part of everyone's life. People in organizations are always learning how to manage their own work better.

Yet you may have noticed that there are times in your organization when everyone is learning, but the organization still can't get the results it wants. Sometimes, learning seems to have no effect at a group level—people learn and learn, and the organization still stays the same.

Organizational learning is learning that results in real changes to the organization. Usually, this involves people building up their ability to work *together* to get the results they really want.

Let me illustrate the difference. Imagine that you and I belong to the same group. We each have things we want to get done, and sometimes we get in each other's way. Each of us *could* learn how to get what we want without help from the other. The trouble with this approach is that what I learn not only makes *my* life easier; it might make *your* life harder, and vice versa. Lots of learning could happen, but the group as a whole won't change.

Organizational learning happens when we work out how to help each other get the results that are really important—to each of us, and to the group as a whole. This may sound easy. It's not! As you can imagine, all sorts of things make it hard for people to work together. The good news is that this kind of learning is both important and exciting. It is often fun, though it can also be painful and difficult. In my experience, the more people try it, the more they like it.

What Results Do *You* Want?

To understand the principles in this Fieldbook, try applying them to something that is important to you and your organization. Take some time to think about where you work. Often everyone is working hard, yet nothing seems to change for the better.

? What is one thing you would like to see change? In the space below, describe a change that would make a real difference in the quality of work life for you and your colleagues. Describe both what you would like, and what is currently happening.

Community (Organizational) Learning in Knith

While reading *Billibonk & the Thorn Patch*, you probably noticed that the groups of animals sometimes demonstrated effective learning habits and other times became stuck in old ways of thinking. In this Fieldbook, we'll look at what encourages learning, and what sometimes makes it difficult.

Most of the time, learning starts with a desire to see a change, like the one you described above. This pattern is shown in the causal loop diagram in Figure 1. When there is a gap between the vision of what you want and how things really are, you work to improve matters. As your success in improving things increases, reality improves, and the gap between vision and reality closes.

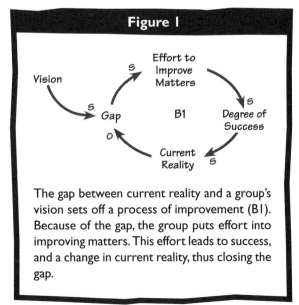

Figure 1

The gap between current reality and a group's vision sets off a process of improvement (B1). Because of the gap, the group puts effort into improving matters. This effort leads to success, and a change in current reality, thus closing the gap.

☼ About Causal Loop Diagrams

Causal loop diagrams, or CLDs, are graphic depictions of systemic structures. The diagrams consist of variables connected by arrows that show the movement of feedback throughout the system. Each arrow is labeled with a sign ("s" or "o") that indicates how one variable influences another. Here's an example of a simple CLD:

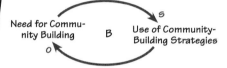

In this diagram, need for community building and use of community-building strategies are the two variables connected by feedback arrows. The "s" on the upper arrow means that when the level of need for community building changes, the use of community-building strategies changes in the *same* direction. For example, if the need increases, the use of strategies also increases. The "o" on the lower arrow means that when use of community-building strategies changes, then the level of need for community building changes in the *opposite* direction. For instance, as use of strategies increases, the need decreases.

Causal loop diagrams are made up of a combination of balancing and reinforcing loops. The simple CLD is an example of a balancing loop, as indicated by the "B" in the center. A *balancing* process tends to keep the system behavior relatively steady overall. In our example, for instance, the two variables balance each other and keep each other under control. A *reinforcing* process, by contrast, drives change in one direction with even more change. Reinforcing processes are recognizable by the uncontrolled or exponential change that they create. The figure below, labeled "R," is a simple example of this kind of dynamic.

In this reinforcing loop, each arrow is labeled with an "s" for same direction of change. To read this diagram, you would say that "as trust increases, so does the willingness to build community, which leads to even more trust."

Balancing and reinforcing processes occur in infinite combinations in the systems we see all around us, including behavior within organizations.

Organizational learning is not about closing one gap and then stopping. When people in a group are learning together, they build up momentum. By the time they have achieved what they wanted (closing the gap), they've learned a lot from working together *and* they've built up a sense of community. Because of this sense, they see new visions of what is possible for themselves, and open up the vision/current reality gap once more. Figure 2 depicts this learning as three reinforcing loops built onto the balancing loop from Figure 1. These reinforcing loops cause the group's success, learning, sense of community, and vision to keep growing, no matter how much the group has already learned. As a result, the more a group learns, the more they *want* to learn.

This is what happened with the elephant herd in *Billibonk & the Thorn Patch*. Once they had learned how to avoid being tricked by monkeys, they decided to establish an evenly balanced relationship with the mice. They had a momentum for learning—and an elephant with momentum is a powerful force!

Recognizing Patterns

You can probably see why organizational learning can be a tough challenge. It's very easy to:

- forget what it is you want to create (or not define your vision clearly in the first place),

- pretend that complex situations are really simple, and

- shy away from discussing important but difficult things.

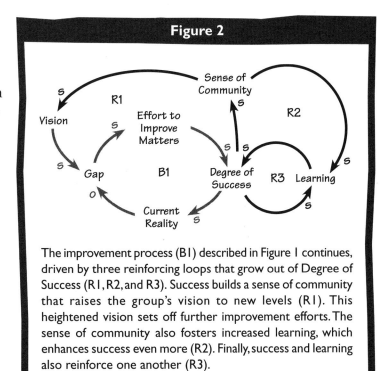

Figure 2

The improvement process (B1) described in Figure 1 continues, driven by three reinforcing loops that grow out of Degree of Success (R1, R2, and R3). Success builds a sense of community that raises the group's vision to new levels (R1). This heightened vision sets off further improvement efforts. The sense of community also fosters increased learning, which enhances success even more (R2). Finally, success and learning also reinforce one another (R3).

Luckily, though, there *is* something that can help us to be better at learning: recognizing behavior patterns that repeat themselves in different settings. Becoming familiar with patterns is especially valuable because it makes complexity easier to handle—if you notice the same overall *pattern* in different situations, you don't have to get caught up in all the little details surrounding the various situations. When you recognize a pattern you have seen before, you can figure out how to apply what you know about the pattern to your own situation.

You may have noticed that some of the things that happened in Knith are also happening in your organization. Let's look at lessons from the story, and how they affected the learning that took place. As well as describing what happened, we will use a series of CLDs to show what happened to the learning that *should* have been going on.

Defining a Problem

As soon as you decide on a vision of what you want that differs from the reality you have got, you create a gap. This gap can inspire you to work to close it. But, the way you *describe* the gap influences how you go about trying to close it.

For example, the elephants in Knith framed the change they wanted in terms of a *solution to a problem*. In their opinion, their problem was, "Too many thorn patches in the jungle." When they defined the problem this way, the obvious answer was to destroy thorns. If they had instead defined the problem as, "We walk into thorn patches too often," they might have thought about the problem in a whole new way.

How Have You Framed the Change *You* Want?
Turn back to your description of the change you want, on page 3.

? Does your description frame the change as a problem that needs solving? If so, what is the problem, and what is the obvious solution your description suggests? Note that framing a problem in this way limits the way you see both the problem and possible solutions.

? Now rework your description so that it does *not* suggest the solution you wrote above. Make your description as open-ended as possible, and try to frame the change in at least two different ways.

Living Systems

One of the first things Billibonk discovered was that you can't treat a living system as if it were dead. The elephants wanted to tear up all the thorns in the jungle, but they didn't realize that the thorns were a living system: Thorn patches housed a community of living things, including mice. As members of a living system, we mice naturally had ideas of our own about our future!

🐾 What Is a System?

A *system* is something made up of parts that interact with each other to work as a whole. Some systems, such as animals, people, and communities, are alive. They have their own goals and desires. Other systems, such as machines, are nonliving. Their parts work together, but only once they have been activated by something that is alive.

Try this: Take four objects out of your pocket or purse. Make sure they are not alive, and then put them on a table. Shove them together. Now move them apart. Put them in a pile. Notice that you can do what you want with them, and they don't change or react. Now imagine trying to do this with four mice! Dealing with living systems is definitely trickier than working with dead ones.

How Do *You* Treat Living Systems?

In many organizations, people treat other people as if they weren't living—as if they were machines, maybe, that exist to serve them. The questions below can help you identify if you have fallen into this way of thinking:

❓ What living systems or communities do you frequently deal with (for example, your customers, your family, your staff)?

[?] Describe a time when you may have treated one of these communities as if it had no opinion of how it wished to be treated.

[?] Living systems don't usually like being treated as if they were dead. How did the group push back at you when you treated it this way?

When a living system fights back, consequences can arise that we never intended or wanted. But these consequences usually don't show up for a while. When they do, they make current reality even worse, so the gaps we thought we'd closed reappear. You can see this process in Figure 3.

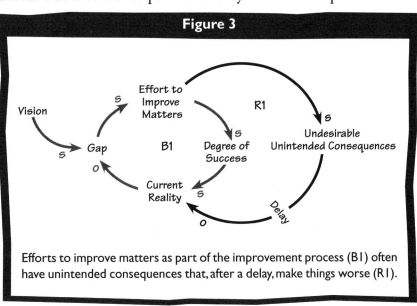

Figure 3

Efforts to improve matters as part of the improvement process (B1) often have unintended consequences that, after a delay, make things worse (R1).

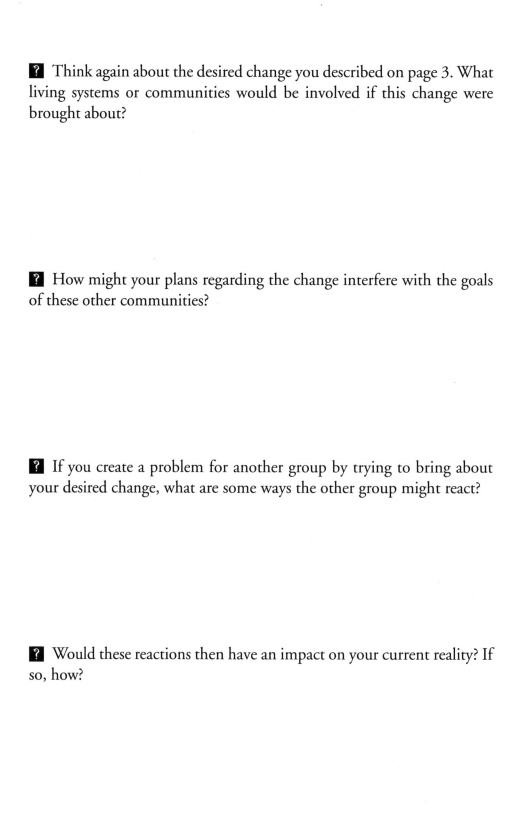

:question: Think again about the desired change you described on page 3. What living systems or communities would be involved if this change were brought about?

:question: How might your plans regarding the change interfere with the goals of these other communities?

:question: If you create a problem for another group by trying to bring about your desired change, what are some ways the other group might react?

:question: Would these reactions then have an impact on your current reality? If so, how?

Reacting vs. Creating

Billibonk's life changed when he realized that he had an impact on his own "luck." He learned that he was part of a living system that wasn't working the way he wanted it to. In particular, his own efforts were actually worsening the problems he was busy trying to solve.

Billibonk discovered that he was part of the problem, and that his own actions had the potential to make the whole system work better.

Many of us are in this situation: We are so busy *reacting* to a system that we don't think about how we can help to *create* the system we want.

Reacting or Creating: How Do You Spend *Your* Time?
Think again about the change you desire.

❓ What are some activities you'll be doing next week because of the change you'd like to see happen? Will these activities mainly cope with things the way they are (reacting), or change the nature of the system itself (creating)?

[?] List five actions you have taken or are likely to take because of the current situation.

[?] Some of the actions you listed may be ones that you keep having to repeat. Why do you think the need for these actions keeps recurring?

[?] List some ways you may be contributing to the pattern of recurrence.

[?] What actions could you take to change the nature of the system itself?

Game Playing

In jungles like Knith, animals spend a lot of time trying to trick one another.

This seems to happen most often when they have nothing to do. Unless they have some larger purpose in mind, animals tend to get caught up in petty competition.

This kind of competition can happen because the community has no vision. When a shared vision is lacking, we often invent games to keep ourselves stimulated. Games become especially tempting when an organization places more emphasis on taking credit for past successes than on working to achieve a new vision. The impact of game playing is shown in Figure 4.

That isn't as bad as it sounds. Sometimes people use games to ensure that certain people don't feel superior to others. In the Knith community, as soon as one animal thinks he or she is wonderful, another comes up with a trick to prove otherwise. When the mice, for instance, began to get puffed up with arrogance, the elephants and monkeys used the Thorn Monster trick to deflate them. Tricks like this help to keep all the animals feeling equal (although at times they also feel pretty foolish!).

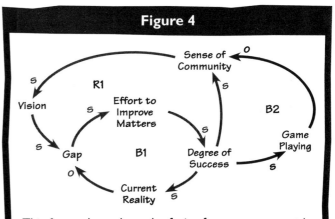

Figure 4

This figure shows how the fruit of success can contain the seeds of failure. As the improvement process (B1) delivers success, people may engage in game playing as they fight over the spoils of that success (B2). Game playing destroys the sense of community; as a result, people lose the shared vision (B3) that previously drove improvements, and they reduce their efforts.

Having a clear, shared purpose has the same effect as tricking each other—and is a lot less humiliating. When people in an organization all have an important purpose in mind that guides their actions, they are usually too focused on that purpose to feel superior to others or to play the "humiliation game."

Games People Play in Your Organization
Game playing (also called "office politics") is a sign that people have taken their minds off the organization's purpose, or that there *is* no purpose in the first place.

[?] Describe a time when game playing affected your ability to get something important done.

[?] Think again about the desired change you described on page 3. Would this change likely inspire others in your organization? Who would *not* be excited about closing the gap you identified?

[?] How might game playing affect your ability to make the change you desire, and have it endure?

[?] What can you do about the impact of game playing?

Things You Can't Discuss

In *Billibonk & the Thorn Patch*, both the elephant herd and the mouse council got into trouble when they didn't talk about what was really important. For instance, I felt that it was wrong for the other mice to go on tricking the elephants, but I was too embarrassed to express my concerns. The other mice knew I wasn't happy, but they ignored me. It was easier for all the mice to ignore the issue than to discuss it.

Many groups fall into patterns like this when they try to talk about things that are really important. You may find that when you go to meetings, you can predict the pattern the meetings will follow: who will say the most, who will withdraw, who will get upset, and so on. Your group may be stuck in a pattern that makes it hard to discuss important things.

If so, you may have noticed that your organization's sense of community is limited. Learning may also be limited, because people won't talk about things they find embarrassing or threatening, even if these issues are crucial to fixing future problems. This dynamic is shown in Figure 5.

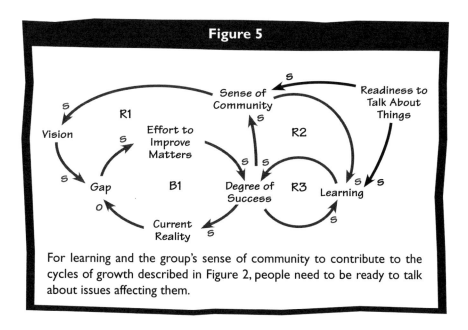

Figure 5

For learning and the group's sense of community to contribute to the cycles of growth described in Figure 2, people need to be ready to talk about issues affecting them.

Undiscussables in Your Organization

? What are some things your group can't discuss? You might recognize them when:
- you or others withdraw from the discussion when these issues arise,
- the issues trigger emotions that you hide,
- you talk about these issues more freely away from the group.

? How will avoiding these undiscussables affect your ability to make the change you want?

? What could you do to make difficult conversations possible?

Conversational Dilemmas

Human systems are complex. When two people interact, they often face dilemmas. At times we have to make a choice between two behaviors, when what we really want is to have both. A common dilemma in conversation is: "Do I tell this person what I think, or do I go easy on his feelings?" During the mouse council meeting, I decided to keep quiet about my concerns so I wouldn't hurt the other mice's feelings. Yollanda and Honka, on the other hand, had an all-out argument when they didn't care about each other's feelings. In both of these situations, the conversation turned out badly because the dilemma was badly managed.

By sharpening your skill at handling conversational dilemmas, you can help your organization talk about things they usually avoid. And by bringing important issues into the open, your organization will remove some of the limitations on its sense of community and its learning. People often know and dislike the feeling of a conversational dilemma. Describing the various sides of the dilemma to others can help to bring important issues into the open. Another skill that's helpful is to think in terms of "both/and" instead of "either/or" while designing a solution to a problem.

The strange thing about these dilemmas is that each option has both good and bad aspects. For example, telling someone else what you think is good because it can help you both understand each other better. However, it can also lead to conflict if you both disagree. (When Yollanda and Honka tried to have an honest talk, their conversation turned into a fight!) It's also good to be considerate of others' feelings—though it can be annoying when you sense that someone else isn't telling you how they really feel!

Dilemmas in *Your* Conversations

Think of the last time you had a really difficult conversation, one that didn't go at all the way you wanted it to. Chances are, the conversation was difficult because of the dilemmas involved in it.

? Write down what you said, what you also wanted to say but didn't, and what the dilemma was that stopped you from saying everything.

Organizational Problems: Three Common Patterns

So far, the CLDs we've looked at suggest that a community's degree of success comes mainly from a combination of both effort and learning from experience. But this isn't the whole story. Life is far more complex, yet the animals in Knith, and most people working in organizations, tend to treat complex problems as if they were simple.

When we oversimplify a problem, we're more likely to experience undesirable consequences of our actions, and these consequences will eat away at any gains made by our short-term successes. You can see this insight in Figure 6.

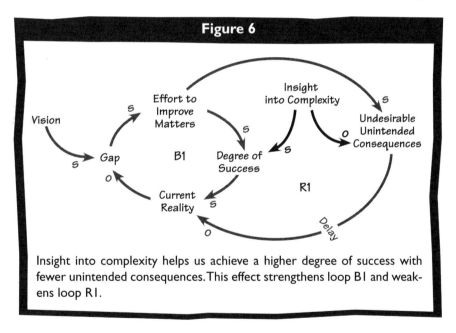

Figure 6

Insight into complexity helps us achieve a higher degree of success with fewer unintended consequences. This effect strengthens loop B1 and weakens loop R1.

How can your organization develop insight into complex situations? Understanding how systems work—especially the patterns of behavior that they typically cause—is an important first step. Over time, you and your organization can learn to recognize these common patterns of behavior. CLDs are especially useful tools for exploring such patterns. Creating your own CLDs can help you and the people in your organization explain to one another what you see as the causal connections behind the problematic behavior patterns you observe.

Some patterns commonly experienced by organizations showed up in *Billibonk & the Thorn Patch*. These could be called Creeping Change, The Trouble with Shared Resources, and Escalation. We'll explore these over the next few pages. (These three patterns may or may not be involved in the situation you want to change. Even if they're not, the following sections may still generate insights that you can use to develop a lasting solution to your issue.)

Creeping Change

As things got more complicated in Knith, I began to get worried about the monkey's scheme, in which they promised to remove the seeds from the yakka-yakka if the elephants would bring them fruit. The scheme was dangerous for the elephants, because it created a problem that would creep up on them over a long period of time—the eventual disappearance of yakka-yakka trees, their main source of food.

When a problem arises quickly (like a snake in a thorn patch), everyone reacts right away. Creeping change often gets ignored. Some of the biggest problems in Knith build up for a long time, and everyone is usually too busy to notice them.

? What is the biggest problem facing *your* organization?

? When did people first notice it?

? Were there signs of the problem before people noticed it? If so, what were they?

? Why didn't people do something about the problem sooner?

? What are some other slow processes that affect your organization? For example, what is happening to:
- your client base?
- service standards?
- staff morale?
- capacity?
- other key variables?

(Don't worry about exact measurements; just write down any basic trends.)

The Trouble with Shared Resources

In *Billibonk & the Thorn Patch*, I finally got the elephants to understand why the monkey scheme failed: The monkeys didn't know how to manage a shared, limited resource (the elephant herd's capacity to pick fruit).

All organizations share many kinds of limited resources: space, time, materials, rewards, and so on. It's not often that there's plenty of everything to go around. One person giving up their share for a while doesn't seem to make any difference; the problem doesn't go away. Organizations need to find ways to manage their limited resources in a sustainable way, so that the resources aren't depleted permanently.

? What essential yet limited resources do people in your organization share?

? How often does the sharing cause conflict? Give an example.

? How is conflict over shared resources managed? Do people "fight it out"? Does one person decide how to allocate a resource, while everyone else gets irritated and thinks it unfair? Is there a way of sharing resources that the whole organization understands and accepts?

Escalation

A common pattern happening in complex systems such as organizations is escalation. Two groups find out that their relationship can get better and better, or worse and worse. This happened in *Billibonk & the Thorn Patch*, when all the animals kept trying to trick each other. Things would have ended badly for everyone if they hadn't decided to help each other instead. (Mice and elephants now get along superbly well!)

People usually act strangely when escalation sets in, especially if it's the kind of escalation that makes the relationship worse. Because both parties keep the problem going, they each blame the other while justifying their own behavior. It's easy to want to be right, but focusing on being right doesn't help things get better.

Escalation can happen between two people, as well as between two groups. The questions below can help you see if you are contributing to a problematic escalation—and may lead to insights for improving a relationship.

? Who seems to be your organization's main competitor or rival?

? What does this competitor do that makes your organization work harder to be better than them?

? What does your group do that makes your competitor work harder to be better than you?

? What common interests do both you and your competitor have that might form the basis for cooperation?

Now that you've seen how some of the lessons learned by the Knith gang might be useful to your own organization, how can you actually apply those lessons?

Because there are several reasons why organizations have trouble learning, there is no *single* action that can make sure that learning happens. You could say that organizational learning is like a three-legged stool. Even if only one leg is short, the stool will be uncomfortable to sit on.

Figure 7 shows the three main "legs" holding up the organizational learning "stool." The various lessons in this Fieldbook can be grouped into the "Creative Orientation," "Managing Complexity," and "Reflective Conversation" "legs" as shown. These legs are broad categories, and encompass many more lessons than are shown in Figure 7. Here, they act as a good start for exploring the exciting world of organizational learning.

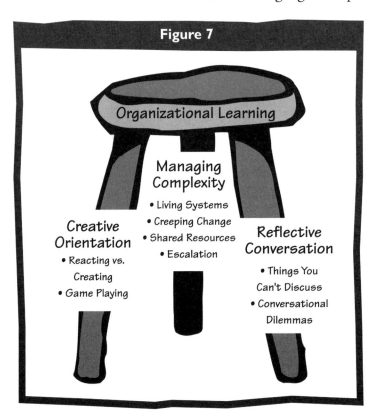

Figure 7

Organizational Learning

Managing Complexity
• Living Systems
• Creeping Change
• Shared Resources
• Escalation

Creative Orientation
• Reacting vs. Creating
• Game Playing

Reflective Conversation
• Things You Can't Discuss
• Conversational Dilemmas

Getting Started

We all know a stool isn't a living system—but an organization is. When you work on one "leg," you'll probably uncover issues that prompt you to work on the other legs. So, while you may start off focusing on one area of change, don't be surprised if you find it important to work on other areas, too.

[?] Take some time now to think about how you might begin improving your organization. What changes would be the most important, in your opinion? Reflect on the thinking you did throughout this Fieldbook, and list the issues you see as the most significant.

🐾 Three "Legs" of Learning

The three legs of organizational learning shown in Figure 7 were suggested by Peter Senge, who wrote *The Fifth Discipline: The Art & Practice of the Learning Organization*. **Creative Orientation** is when people work to create what they want rather than react to what happens around them. To do this, you hold a vision in mind of what you want to create, and master the dynamics of the creative process—a difficult task at times. **Managing Complexity** refers to the ability to understand the world and our own part in it. To take this approach, you have to work hard to fight the tendency to oversimplify and blame others for things you don't like. Finally, **Reflective Conversation** refers to a group's ability to have deep talks about their problems and share their different views of it, all while building themselves into a strong community.

Important Practice

One of the best ways to learn about learning is to teach someone else. This someone else can be anyone, though it's best if he or she knows less than you do!

Try this: Read *Billibonk & the Thorn Patch* to a child, and see how much you can learn together from the story. Here are some tips for making it work.

Share the Reading

Depending on the ability of the child you're reading to, take turns reading paragraphs or chapters. A fun alternative is to share the animals' voices—the child could say everything that one character says, and even use a funny or strange voice if he or she chose. Some children find the footnotes in the story distracting. If this is the case, just skip over them. The child may enjoy rereading the book later, including the footnotes.

Ask Questions

Every now and then, ask questions to encourage the child to compare the characters' experiences with his or her own. Don't worry about asking questions after each chapter; some children may simply want to find out how the story ends. Possible questions for each chapter include:

1. Why do you think Frankl said Billibonk had courage to get out of the thorns? When have *you* been courageous like Billibonk?
2. What do you think of the elephants' plan to tear up all the thorn patches?
3. Why do you think Honka and Yollanda ended up having an argument about the elephants' plan? When have *you* gotten into arguments like this?
4. What do you think the mice will do after hearing about the elephants' plan to tear up the thorn patches? What would *you* do if you were them?

5. Have you ever been tricked, like the elephants and the "Thorn Monster"?

6. What do you think is going to happen next, now that the monkeys have involved the elephants in the yakka-yakka and fruit plan?

7. A lot of plants and animals need each other. Can you think of other plants and animals, besides the yakka-yakka and elephants in the story, that need each other?

8. Why didn't the monkeys' scheme to make the elephants bring them fruit keep working?

9. Do you think Yollanda should have kept trying to trick the elephants?

10. Why didn't the other mice want to listen to Frankl's concerns about tricking the elephants again?

11. How do you think the mice are feeling, after the Thorn Monster scare?

12. Why do you think Frankl is worried about the animals' continuing to trick each other?

13. Frankl was happy to be tricked, because it helped him learn an important lesson. Have you ever been happy to be wrong? If so, when?

14. What could have happened if the animals hadn't sorted out their problems with each other?

15. What did you think of the story?

Share Your Own Stories
Children enjoy hearing adults tell stories of their own lives, especially stories that disclose information not obvious to others. Share examples of lessons you've learned, and ask the child to share some of his or hers.

A Goodbye

Happy learning as you bring your new insights to your organization! I hope you learned a lot by thinking over the questions in the Fieldbook—and that you had fun, too! If you have other ideas about how to use *Billibonk & the Thorn Patch*, or if something in the Fieldbook worked particularly well for you, feel free to tell me. There are no fax machines or phones in Knith, but if you want to get in touch you can reach Phil Ramsey by email at the following address: P.L.Ramsey@massey.ac.nz.